FORTY DAYS OF

HOPE

Written and Edited by MacKenzie Wilson

A Scripture Journal

COMMON
ENGLIƧH
BIBLE

Nashville

FORTY DAYS OF HOPE:
A SCRIPTURE JOURNAL

Copyright © 2015 by Common English Bible

All rights reserved.

This book is printed on acid-free paper.

ISBN 978-1-60926-193-1

15 16 17 18 19 20 21 22 23 24—10 9 8 7 6 5 4 3 2 1

MANUFACTURED IN CHINA

INTRODUCTION

Hope is an essential part of the Christian faith, but for many people it can seem daunting to one day put on the garment of hope and steadfastly carry it wherever they go. For many of us, hope is fleeting and hard to hold on to for the long run. But maybe hope as an overnight sensation isn't the whole picture of what God is calling us to.

This book won't provide one piece of scripture that perfectly sums up hope and teaches you how to vigorously abide in it. Instead, this book can be the starting point for finding hope in all the things that Christ has placed before us.

The scriptures in this book are road signs and landmarks on the journey of hope, because hope isn't a destination but rather a long, winding, and beautiful journey—a journey full of wrong turns, breathtaking lookouts, dark woods, and a lot of pit stops along the way. It's a journey of finding hope and joy in the moments we often overlook. The scriptures throughout this book will help you to reflect and meditate upon hope in the things this world doesn't often value like diversity, the desert, humility, and poverty. They will give momentum to your journey of finding hope in community, our churches, love, and creation.

Imagine the impact that would follow if every day we woke up and said, "Today I choose to see hope in _____." This book will help you to fill in that blank for the next forty days. In these forty days of hope, may you encounter God every day through meditating on God's word. May this process be one where we let hope transform our hearts, move us to love deeper, be our praise and our worship, and remind us who we are in Christ. May these forty days be our cornerstone for a lifetime of hope.

DAY 1

Isaiah 9:2-7

The people walking in darkness have seen a great light.
  On those living in a pitch-dark land,
    light has dawned.
You have made the nation great;
  you have increased its joy.
They rejoiced before you as with joy at the harvest,
  as those who divide plunder rejoice.
As on the day of Midian,
  you've shattered the yoke that burdened them,
  the staff on their shoulders,
  and the rod of their oppressor.
Because every boot of the thundering warriors,
  and every garment rolled in blood
  will be burned, fuel for the fire.
A child is born to us, a son is given to us,
  and authority will be on his shoulders.
  He will be named
  Wonderful Counselor, Mighty God,
  Eternal Father, Prince of Peace.
There will be vast authority and endless peace
  for David's throne and for his kingdom,
  establishing and sustaining it

with justice and righteousness
  now and forever.
The zeal of the LORD of heavenly forces will do this.

John 1:1-14

In the beginning was the Word
  and the Word was with God
  and the Word was God.
The Word was with God in the beginning.
Everything came into being through the Word,
  and without the Word
  nothing came into being.
What came into being
  through the Word was life,
  and the life was the light for all people.
The light shines in the darkness,
  and the darkness doesn't extinguish the light.
A man named John was sent from God. He came as a witness to testify concerning the light, so that through him everyone would believe in the light. He himself wasn't the light, but his mission was to testify concerning the light.
The true light that shines on all people
  was coming into the world.
The light was in the world,
  and the world came into being through the light,
    but the world didn't recognize the light.
The light came to his own people,
  and his own people didn't welcome him.
But those who did welcome him,
  those who believed in his name,

he authorized to become God's children,
  born not from blood
  nor from human desire or passion,
  but born from God.
The Word became flesh
  and made his home among us.
We have seen his glory,
  glory like that of a father's only son,
    full of grace and truth.

John 8:12

Jesus spoke to the people again, saying, "I am the light of the world. Whoever follows me won't walk in darkness but will have the light of life."

MEDITATION

Jesus is God with us. He has come to shine light into the darkness and turn our despair into joy. Where might God be shining light into the darkness of our world? Where might God be shining light into the darkness of your life?

_____

_____

Day 1

Day 2

Matthew 4:1-11

Then the Spirit led Jesus up into the wilderness so that the devil might tempt him. After Jesus had fasted for forty days and forty nights, he was starving. The tempter came to him and said, "Since you are God's Son, command these stones to become bread."

Jesus replied, "It's written, *People won't live only by bread, but by every word spoken by God.*"

After that the devil brought him into the holy city and stood him at the highest point of the temple. He said to him, "Since you are God's Son, throw yourself down; for it is written, *I will command my angels concerning you, and they will take you up in their hands so that you won't hit your foot on a stone.*"

Jesus replied, "Again it's written, *Don't test the Lord your God.*"

Then the devil brought him to a very high mountain and showed him all the kingdoms of the world and their glory. He said, "I'll give you all these if you bow down and worship me."

Jesus responded, "Go away, Satan, because it's written, *You will worship the Lord your God and serve only him.*" The devil left him, and angels came and took care of him.

Hosea 2:14-20

Therefore, I will charm her,
  and bring her into the desert,
  and speak tenderly to her heart.
From there I will give her vineyards,
  and make the Achor Valley a door of hope.
  There she will respond to me
  as in the days of her youth,
  like the time when she came
    out of the land of Egypt.
On that day, says the LORD, you will call me, "My husband," and no longer will you call me, "My Lord." I will take away the names of the Baals from her mouth, and they will not be mentioned by name anymore. On that day, I will make a covenant for them with the wild animals, the birds in the sky, and the creeping creatures of the fertile ground. I will do away with the bow, the sword, and war from the land; I will make you lie down in safety.

I will take you for my wife forever;
  I will take you for my wife
    in righteousness and in justice,
    in devoted love, and in mercy.
I will take you for my wife in faithfulness;
  and you will know the LORD.

Psalm 126:3-5

Yes, the LORD has done great things for us,
  and we are overjoyed.

LORD, change our circumstances for the better,
  like dry streams in the desert waste!
Let those who plant with tears
  reap the harvest with joyful shouts.

MEDITATION

*Jesus spent forty days in the wilderness
in temptation yet remained steadfast
in the Father. How can we find hope when
we are tempted in the desert, in seasons
of our own wilderness?*

_____

_____

_____

_____

_____

_____

_____

_____

_____

_____

DAY 3

Luke 10:17-20

The seventy-two returned joyously, saying, "Lord, even the demons submit themselves to us in your name."

Jesus replied, "I saw Satan fall from heaven like lightning. Look, I have given you authority to crush snakes and scorpions underfoot. I have given you authority over all the power of the enemy. Nothing will harm you. Nevertheless, don't rejoice because the spirits submit to you. Rejoice instead that your names are written in heaven."

1 Peter 2:4-10

Now you are coming to him as to a living stone. Even though this stone was rejected by humans, from God's perspective it is chosen, valuable. You yourselves are being built like living stones into a spiritual temple. You are being made into a holy priesthood to offer up spiritual sacrifices that are acceptable to God through Jesus Christ. Thus it is written in scripture, *Look! I am laying a cornerstone in Zion, chosen, valuable. The person who believes in him will never be shamed.* So God honors you who believe. For those who refuse to believe, though, the stone the builders tossed aside has become the capstone. This is a stone that makes people stumble and a rock that makes them fall. Because they refuse to believe in the word, they stumble. Indeed, this is the end to which they were appointed. But you are a chosen race, a royal priesthood, a holy nation, a people who are God's own possession. You have become this people so that you may speak of the wonderful acts of the one who called you out of darkness into his amazing light. Once you weren't a people, but now you are God's people. Once you hadn't received mercy, but now you have received mercy.

Genesis 1:27

God created humanity in God's own image,
in the divine image God created them,
male and female God created them.

MEDITATION

*There is hope in belonging to a God who has
written your name in heaven. There is joy
in belonging to a God who has chosen you.
How can you find hope in belonging?*

DAY 4

Psalm 119:97-104, 161-168

I love your Instruction!
  I think about it constantly.
Your commandment makes me wiser than my enemies
  because it is always with me.
I have greater insight than all my teachers
  because I contemplate your laws.
I have more understanding than the elders
  because I guard your precepts.
I haven't set my feet on any evil path
  so I can make sure to keep your word.
I haven't deviated from any of your rules
  because you are the one who has taught me.
Your word is so pleasing to my taste buds—
  it's sweeter than honey in my mouth!
I'm studying your precepts—
  that's why I hate every false path.

Rulers oppress me without cause,
  but my heart honors what you've said.
I'm overjoyed at your word,
  like someone who finds great treasure.
I hate, I absolutely despise, what is false,
  but I'm in love with your Instruction.

I praise you seven times a day
  for your righteous rules.
The people who love your Instruction enjoy peace—
  and lots of it.
  There's no stumbling for them!
LORD, I wait for your saving help.
  I do what you've commanded.
I keep your laws;
  I love them so much!
I keep your precepts and your laws
  because all my ways are seen by you.

2 Timothy 3:14-17

But you must continue with the things you have learned and found convincing. You know who taught you. Since childhood you have known the holy scriptures that help you to be wise in a way that leads to salvation through faith that is in Christ Jesus. Every scripture is inspired by God and is useful for teaching, for showing mistakes, for correcting, and for training character, so that the person who belongs to God can be equipped to do everything that is good.

Jeremiah 15:16

When your words turned up, I feasted on them;
  and they became my joy, the delight of my heart,
    because I belong to you,
    LORD God of heavenly forces.

MEDITATION

*The word of God brings joy to our lips
and refreshes our spirits. How can you,
like the psalmist, take great joy and
hope in God's Instruction?*

_____

_____

_____

_____

_____

_____

_____

_____

_____

_____

_____

_____

_____

_____

_____

_____

Day 5

Romans 12:3-22

Because of the grace that God gave me, I can say to each one of you: don't think of yourself more highly than you ought to think. Instead, be reasonable since God has measured out a portion of faith to each one of you. We have many parts in one body, but the parts don't all have the same function. In the same way, though there are many of us, we are one body in Christ, and individually we belong to each other. We have different gifts that are consistent with God's grace that has been given to us. If your gift is prophecy, you should prophesy in proportion to your faith. If your gift is service, devote yourself to serving. If your gift is teaching, devote yourself to teaching. If your gift is encouragement, devote yourself to encouraging. The one giving should do it with no strings attached. The leader should lead with passion. The one showing mercy should be cheerful.

Love should be shown without pretending. Hate evil, and hold on to what is good. Love each other like the members of your family. Be the best at showing honor to each other. Don't hesitate to be enthusiastic—be on fire in the Spirit as you serve the Lord! Be happy in your hope, stand your ground when you're in trouble, and devote yourselves to prayer. Contribute to the needs of God's people, and welcome strangers into your home. Bless people who harass you—bless and don't curse them. Be happy with those who are happy, and cry with those who are crying. Consider everyone as equal, and don't think that you're better than anyone else. Instead, associate with people who have no status. Don't think that you're so smart. Don't pay back anyone for their evil actions with evil actions, but show respect for what everyone else believes is good.

If possible, to the best of your ability, live at peace with all people. Don't try to get revenge for yourselves, my dear friends, but leave room for God's wrath. It is written, *Revenge belongs to me; I will pay it back, says the Lord.* Instead, *If your enemy is hungry, feed him; if he is thirsty, give him a drink. By doing this, you will pile burning coals of fire upon his head.* Don't be defeated by evil, but defeat evil with good.

Hebrews 10:24-25

And let us consider each other carefully for the purpose of sparking love and good deeds. Don't stop meeting together with other believers, which some people have gotten into the habit of doing. Instead, encourage each other, especially as you see the day drawing near.

MEDITATION

*We all are a part of the body of Christ.
How can we find hope in one another?
How can we encourage one another
onward toward Christ?*

_____

_____

_____

_____

_____

_____

_____

_____

_____

_____

_____

_____

_____

_____

DAY 6

Judges 6:11-17

Then the LORD's messenger came and sat under the oak at Ophrah that belonged to Joash the Abiezrite. His son Gideon was threshing wheat in a winepress to hide it from the Midianites. The LORD's messenger appeared to him and said, "The LORD is with you, mighty warrior!"

But Gideon replied to him, "With all due respect, my Lord, if the LORD is with us, why has all this happened to us? Where are all his amazing works that our ancestors recounted to us, saying, 'Didn't the LORD bring us up from Egypt?' But now the LORD has abandoned us and allowed Midian to overpower us."

Then the LORD turned to him and said, "You have strength, so go and rescue Israel from the power of Midian. Am I not personally sending you?"

But again Gideon said to him, "With all due respect, my Lord, how can I rescue Israel? My clan is the weakest in Manasseh, and I'm the youngest in my household."

The LORD replied, "Because I'm with you, you'll defeat the Midianites as if they were just one person."

Then Gideon said to him, "If I've gained your approval, please show me a sign that it's really you speaking with me."

Hebrews 11:32-34

What more can I say? I would run out of time if I told you about Gideon, Barak, Samson, Jephthah, David, Samuel, and the prophets. Through faith they conquered kingdoms, brought about justice, realized promises, shut the mouths of lions, put out raging fires, escaped from the edge of the sword, found strength in weakness, were mighty in war, and routed foreign armies.

2 Corinthians 12:10

Therefore, I'm all right with weaknesses, insults, disasters, harassments, and stressful situations for the sake of Christ, because when I'm weak, then I'm strong.

1 Corinthians 1:27

But God chose what the world considers foolish to shame the wise. God chose what the world considers weak to shame the strong.

MEDITATION

In God's kingdom, the weak are made strong.
Pray and thank God for your weaknesses.
Reflect on how God's strength can
be displayed through your weakness.

_____

_____

_____

_____

_____

_____

_____

_____

_____

_____

_____

_____

_____

_____

Day 7

James 1:2-12

My brothers and sisters, think of the various tests you encounter as occasions for joy. After all, you know that the testing of your faith produces endurance. Let this endurance complete its work so that you may be fully mature, complete, and lacking in nothing. But anyone who needs wisdom should ask God, whose very nature is to give to everyone without a second thought, without keeping score. Wisdom will certainly be given to those who ask. Whoever asks shouldn't hesitate. They should ask in faith, without doubting. Whoever doubts is like the surf of the sea, tossed and turned by the wind. People like that should never imagine that they will receive anything from the Lord. They are double-minded, unstable in all their ways.

Brothers and sisters who are poor should find satisfaction in their high status. Those who are wealthy should find satisfaction in their low status, because they will die off like wildflowers. The sun rises with its scorching heat and dries up the grass so that its flowers fall and its beauty is lost. Just like that, in the midst of their daily lives, the wealthy will waste away. Those who stand firm during testing are blessed. They are tried and true. They will receive the life God has promised to those who love him as their reward.

1 Peter 1:6-9

You now rejoice in this hope, even if it's necessary for you to be distressed for a short time by various trials. This is necessary so that your faith may be found genuine. (Your faith is more valuable than gold, which will be destroyed even though it is itself tested by fire.) Your genuine faith will result in praise, glory, and honor for you when Jesus Christ is revealed. Although you've never seen him, you love him. Even though you don't see him now, you trust him and so rejoice with a glorious joy that is too much for words. You are receiving the goal of your faith: your salvation.

1 Peter 5:6-11

Therefore, humble yourselves under God's power so that he may raise you up in the last day. Throw all your anxiety onto him, because he cares about you. Be clearheaded. Keep alert. Your accuser, the devil, is on the prowl like a roaring lion, seeking someone to devour. Resist him, standing firm in the faith. Do so in the knowledge that your fellow believers are enduring the same suffering throughout the world. After you have suffered for a little while, the God of all grace, the one who called you into his eternal glory in Christ Jesus, will himself restore, empower, strengthen, and establish you. To him be power forever and always. Amen.

MEDITATION

*We are told to think of the various tests
we encounter as occasions for joy. This can
be extremely difficult, but how can we stand
firm during testing? How can we find hope
and confidence in the God of all grace?*

_____

_____

_____

_____

_____

_____

_____

_____

_____

_____

_____

_____

_____

DAY 8

2 Corinthians 9:5-15

This is why I thought it was necessary to encourage the brothers to go to you ahead of time and arrange in advance the generous gift you have already promised. I want it to be a real gift from you. I don't want you to feel like you are being forced to give anything. What I mean is this: the one who sows a small number of seeds will also reap a small crop, and the one who sows a generous amount of seeds will also reap a generous crop.

Everyone should give whatever they have decided in their heart. They shouldn't give with hesitation or because of pressure. God loves a cheerful giver. God has the power to provide you with more than enough of every kind of grace. That way, you will have everything you need always and in everything to provide more than enough for every kind of good work. As it is written, *He scattered everywhere; he gave to the needy; his righteousness remains forever.*

The one who supplies seed for planting and bread for eating will supply and multiply your seed and will increase your crop, which is righteousness. You will be made rich in every way so that you can be generous in every way. Such generosity produces thanksgiving to God through us. Your ministry of this service to God's people isn't only fully meeting their needs but it is also multiplying in many expressions of thanksgiving to God. They will give honor to God for your obedience to your confession of Christ's gospel. They will do this because this service provides evidence of your obedience, and because of your generosity in sharing with them and with everyone. They will also pray for you, and they will care deeply for you because of the outstanding grace that God has given to you. Thank God for his gift that words can't describe!

Matthew 6:1-4

"Be careful that you don't practice your religion in front of people to draw their attention. If you do, you will have no reward from your Father who is in heaven.

"Whenever you give to the poor, don't blow your trumpet as the hypocrites do in the synagogues and in the streets so that they may get praise from people. I assure you, that's the only reward they'll get. But when you give to the poor, don't let your left hand know what your right hand is doing so that you may give to the poor in secret. Your Father who sees what you do in secret will reward you."

Proverbs 11:24-25

Those who give generously receive more,
but those who are stingy with what is appropriate
will grow needy.

Generous persons will prosper;
  those who refresh others will themselves be
  refreshed.

MEDITATION

*God loves a cheerful giver. Are you
giving of your self, time, finances,
and possessions? Does your giving
reflect the hope you have in Christ?
How might God be calling you to give?*

_____

_____

_____

_____

_____

_____

_____

_____

_____

DAY 9

1 Thessalonians 5:16-18

Rejoice always. Pray continually. Give thanks in every situation because this is God's will for you in Christ Jesus.

Luke 6:12-19

During that time, Jesus went out to the mountain to pray, and he prayed to God all night long. At daybreak, he called together his disciples. He chose twelve of them whom he called apostles: Simon, whom he named Peter; his brother Andrew; James; John; Philip; Bartholomew; Matthew; Thomas; James the son of Alphaeus; Simon, who was called a zealot; Judas the son of James; and Judas Iscariot, who became a traitor.

Jesus came down from the mountain with them and stood on a large area of level ground. A great company of his disciples and a huge crowd of people from all around Judea and Jerusalem and the area around Tyre and Sidon joined him there. They came to hear him and to be healed from their diseases, and those bothered by unclean spirits were healed. The whole crowd wanted to touch him, because power was going out from him and he was healing everyone.

Luke 18:1-8

Jesus was telling them a parable about their need to pray continuously and not to be discouraged. He said, "In a certain city there was a judge who neither feared God nor respected people. In that city there was a widow who kept coming to him, asking, 'Give me justice in this case against my adversary.' For a while he refused but finally said to himself, I don't fear God or respect people, but I will give this widow justice because she keeps bothering me. Otherwise, there will be no end to her coming here and embarrassing me." The Lord said, "Listen to what the unjust judge says. Won't God provide justice to his chosen people who cry out to him day and night? Will he be slow to help them? I tell you, he will give them justice quickly. But when the Human One comes, will he find faithfulness on earth?"

Luke 11:1-4

Jesus was praying in a certain place. When he finished, one of his disciples said, "Lord, teach us to pray, just as John taught his disciples."

Jesus told them, "When you pray, say:
'Father, uphold the holiness of your name.
Bring in your kingdom.
Give us the bread we need for today.
Forgive us our sins,
   for we also forgive everyone who has wronged us.
And don't lead us into temptation.'"

MEDITATION

*We are called to rejoice in everything
and to pray continuously. Reflect on the
prayer life of Jesus. What can Jesus
teach us about how to pray?*

_____

_____

_____

_____

_____

_____

_____

_____

_____

_____

_____

_____

_____

_____

DAY 10

Mark 1:16-20

As Jesus passed alongside the Galilee Sea, he saw two brothers, Simon and Andrew, throwing fishing nets into the sea, for they were fishermen. "Come, follow me," he said, "and I'll show you how to fish for people." Right away, they left their nets and followed him. After going a little farther, he saw James and John, Zebedee's sons, in their boat repairing the fishing nets. At that very moment he called them. They followed him, leaving their father Zebedee in the boat with the hired workers.

Ephesians 4:11-16

He gave some apostles, some prophets, some evangelists, and some pastors and teachers. His purpose was to equip God's people for the work of serving and building up the body of Christ until we all reach the unity of faith and knowledge of God's Son. God's goal is for us to become mature adults—to be fully grown, measured by the standard of the fullness of Christ. As a result, we aren't supposed to be infants any longer who can be tossed and blown around by every wind that comes from teaching with deceitful scheming and the tricks people play to deliberately mislead others. Instead, by speaking the truth with love, let's grow in every way into Christ, who is the head. The whole body grows from him, as it is joined and held together by all the supporting ligaments. The body makes itself grow in that it builds itself up with love as each one does its part.

Matthew 28:16-20

Now the eleven disciples went to Galilee, to the mountain where Jesus told them to go. When they saw him, they worshipped him, but some doubted. Jesus came near and spoke to them, "I've received all authority in heaven and on earth. Therefore, go and make disciples of all nations, baptizing them in the name of the Father and of the Son and of the Holy Spirit, teaching them to obey everything that I've commanded you. Look, I myself will be with you every day until the end of this present age."

～ MEDITATION ～

As Christ's disciples, we have great hope through the great commission. Whom might God be asking you to teach and disciple? How can we share the hope that Christ has given us with others through discipleship?

DAY 11

Luke 15:11-32

Jesus said, "A certain man had two sons. The younger son said to his father, 'Father, give me my share of the inheritance.' Then the father divided his estate between them. Soon afterward, the younger son gathered everything together and took a trip to a land far away. There, he wasted his wealth through extravagant living.

"When he had used up his resources, a severe food shortage arose in that country and he began to be in need. He hired himself out to one of the citizens of that country, who sent him into his fields to feed pigs. He longed to eat his fill from what the pigs ate, but no one gave him anything. When he came to his senses, he said, 'How many of my father's hired hands have more than enough food, but I'm starving to death! I will get up and go to my father, and say to him, "Father, I have sinned against heaven and against you. I no longer deserve to be called your son. Take me on as one of your hired hands."' So he got up and went to his father.

"While he was still a long way off, his father saw him and was moved with compassion. His father ran to him, hugged him, and kissed him. Then his son said, 'Father, I have sinned against heaven and against you. I no longer deserve to be called your son.' But the father said to his servants, 'Quickly, bring out the best robe and put it on him! Put a ring on his finger and sandals on his feet! Fetch the fattened calf and slaughter it. We must celebrate with feasting because this son of mine was dead and has come back to life! He was lost and is found!' And they began to celebrate.

"Now his older son was in the field. Coming in from the field, he approached the house and heard music and dancing. He called one of the servants and asked what was going on. The servant replied, 'Your brother has arrived, and your father has slaughtered the fattened calf because he received his son back safe and sound.' Then the older son was furious and didn't want to enter in, but his father came out and begged him. He answered his father, 'Look, I've served you all these years, and I never disobeyed your instruction. Yet you've never given me as much as a young goat so I could celebrate with my friends. But when this son of yours returned, after gobbling up your estate on prostitutes, you slaughtered the fattened calf for him.' Then his father said, 'Son, you are always with me, and everything I have is yours. But we had to celebrate and be glad because this brother of yours was dead and is alive. He was lost and is found.'"

MEDITATION

Reflect on times when you've felt dirty or unworthy like the prodigal son. God waits with open arms for us to return home. God celebrates forgiveness.

DAY 12

John 10:11-18

"I am the good shepherd. The good shepherd lays down his life for the sheep. When the hired hand sees the wolf coming, he leaves the sheep and runs away. That's because he isn't the shepherd; the sheep aren't really his. So the wolf attacks the sheep and scatters them. He's only a hired hand and the sheep don't matter to him.

"I am the good shepherd. I know my own sheep and they know me, just as the Father knows me and I know the Father. I give up my life for the sheep. I have other sheep that don't belong to this sheep pen. I must lead them too. They will listen to my voice and there will be one flock, with one shepherd.

"This is why the Father loves me: I give up my life so that I can take it up again. No one takes it from me, but I give it up because I want to. I have the right to give it up, and I have the right to take it up again. I received this commandment from my Father."

Matthew 18:10-14

"Be careful that you don't look down on one of these little ones. I say to you that their angels in heaven are always looking into the face of my Father who is in heaven. What do you think? If someone had one hundred sheep and one of them wandered off, wouldn't he leave the ninety-nine on the hillsides and go in search for the one that wandered off? If he finds it, I assure you that he is happier about having that one sheep than about the ninety-nine who didn't wander off. In the same way, my Father who is in heaven doesn't want to lose one of these little ones."

Psalm 100:1-5

Shout triumphantly to the LORD, all the earth!
　Serve the LORD with celebration!
　Come before him with shouts of joy!
Know that the LORD is God—
　he made us; we belong to him.
　We are his people, the sheep of his own pasture.
Enter his gates with thanks;
　enter his courtyards with praise!
　Thank him! Bless his name!
Because the LORD is good, his loyal love lasts forever;
　his faithfulness lasts generation after generation.

MEDITATION

We belong to Jesus. What great hope there is in being the good shepherd's sheep. Reflect on times in your life when Jesus has left the flock to search for the one lost sheep.

_____

_____

_____

_____

_____

_____

_____

_____

_____

_____

_____

_____

_____

_____

DAY 13

John 1:24-34

Those sent by the Pharisees asked, "Why do you baptize if you aren't the Christ, nor Elijah, nor the prophet?"

John answered, "I baptize with water. Someone greater stands among you, whom you don't recognize. He comes after me, but I'm not worthy to untie his sandal straps." This encounter took place across the Jordan in Bethany where John was baptizing.

The next day John saw Jesus coming toward him and said, "Look! The Lamb of God who takes away the sin of the world! This is the one about whom I said, 'He who comes after me is really greater than me because he existed before me.' Even I didn't recognize him, but I came baptizing with water so that he might be made known to Israel." John testified, "I saw the Spirit coming down from heaven like a dove, and it rested on him. Even I didn't recognize him, but the one who sent me to baptize with water said to me, 'The one on whom you see the Spirit coming down and resting is the one who baptizes with the Holy Spirit.' I have seen and testified that this one is God's Son."

Romans 6:3-11

Or don't you know that all who were baptized into Christ Jesus were baptized into his death? Therefore, we were buried together with him through baptism into his death, so that just as Christ was raised from the dead through the glory of the Father, we too can walk in newness of life. If we were united together in a death like his, we will also be united together in a resurrection like his. This is what we know: the person that we used to be was crucified with him in order to get rid of the corpse that had been controlled by sin. That way we wouldn't be slaves to sin anymore, because a person who has died has been freed from sin's power. But if we died with Christ, we have faith that we will also live with him. We know that Christ has been raised from the dead and he will never die again. Death no longer has power over him. He died to sin once and for all with his death, but he lives for God with his life. In the same way, you also should consider yourselves dead to sin but alive for God in Christ Jesus.

Galatians 3:26-28

You are all God's children through faith in Christ Jesus. All of you who were baptized into Christ have clothed yourselves with Christ. There is neither Jew nor Greek; there is neither slave nor free; nor is there male and female, for you are all one in Christ Jesus.

MEDITATION

Spend time reflecting on your baptism.
When we are baptized into Christ,
we are made new and free.
Are you living into your freedom?

_____

_____

_____

_____

_____

_____

_____

_____

_____

_____

_____

_____

_____

_____

DAY 14

Matthew 14:22-33

Right then, Jesus made the disciples get into the boat and go ahead to the other side of the lake while he dismissed the crowds. When he sent them away, he went up onto a mountain by himself to pray. Evening came and he was alone. Meanwhile, the boat, fighting a strong headwind, was being battered by the waves and was already far away from land. Very early in the morning he came to his disciples, walking on the lake. When the disciples saw him walking on the lake, they were terrified and said, "It's a ghost!" They were so frightened they screamed.

Just then Jesus spoke to them, "Be encouraged! It's me. Don't be afraid."

Peter replied, "Lord, if it's you, order me to come to you on the water."

And Jesus said, "Come."

Then Peter got out of the boat and was walking on the water toward Jesus. But when Peter saw the strong wind, he became frightened. As he began to sink, he shouted, "Lord, rescue me!"

Jesus immediately reached out and grabbed him, saying, "You man of weak faith! Why did you begin to have doubts?" When they got into the boat, the wind settled down.

Then those in the boat worshipped Jesus and said, "You must be God's Son!"

Joshua 1:7-9

"Be very brave and strong as you carefully obey all of the Instruction that Moses my servant commanded you. Don't deviate even a bit from it, either to the right or left. Then you will have success wherever you go. Never stop speaking about this Instruction scroll. Recite it day and night so you can carefully obey everything written in it. Then you will accomplish your objectives and you will succeed. I've commanded you to be brave and strong, haven't I? Don't be alarmed or terrified, because the LORD your God is with you wherever you go."

Hebrews 11:1-6

Faith is the reality of what we hope for, the proof of what we don't see. The elders in the past were approved because they showed faith.

By faith we understand that the universe has been created by a word from God so that the visible came into existence from the invisible.

By faith Abel offered a better sacrifice to God than Cain, which showed that he was righteous, since God gave approval to him for his gift. Though he died, he's still speaking through faith.

By faith Enoch was taken up so that he didn't see death, and *he wasn't found because God took him up.* He was given approval for having pleased God before he was taken up. It's impossible to please God without faith because the one who draws near to God must believe that he exists and that he rewards people who try to find him.

MEDITATION

We are called to be brave and strong in getting out of the boat. In which areas of your life is God calling you to step out in faith?

_____

_____

_____

_____

_____

_____

_____

_____

_____

DAY 15

John 6:26-35

Jesus replied, "I assure you that you are looking for me not because you saw miraculous signs but because you ate all the food you wanted. Don't work for the food that doesn't last but for the food that endures for eternal life, which the Human One will give you. God the Father has confirmed him as his agent to give life."

They asked, "What must we do in order to accomplish what God requires?"

Jesus replied, "This is what God requires, that you believe in him whom God sent."

They asked, "What miraculous sign will you do, that we can see and believe you? What will you do? Our ancestors ate manna in the wilderness, just as it is written, *He gave them bread from heaven to eat.*"

Jesus told them, "I assure you, it wasn't Moses who gave the bread from heaven to you, but my Father gives you the true bread from heaven. The bread of God is the one who comes down from heaven and gives life to the world."

They said, "Sir, give us this bread all the time!"

Jesus replied, "I am the bread of life. Whoever comes to me will never go hungry, and whoever believes in me will never be thirsty."

Isaiah 55:1-2

All of you who are thirsty, come to the water!
Whoever has no money, come, buy food and eat!
Without money, at no cost, buy wine and milk!
Why spend money for what isn't food,
    and your earnings for what doesn't satisfy?
Listen carefully to me and eat what is good;
    enjoy the richest of feasts.

Psalm 107:4-9

Some of the redeemed had wandered into the desert,
    into the wasteland.
    They couldn't find their way to a city or town.
They were hungry and thirsty;
    their lives were slipping away.
So they cried out to the LORD in their distress,
    and God delivered them
        from their desperate circumstances.
    God led them straight to human habitation.
Let them thank the LORD for his faithful love
    and his wondrous works for all people,
    because God satisfied the one
        who was parched with thirst,
    and he filled up the hungry with good things!

MEDITATION

*Jesus is the bread of life, but often we look
for satisfaction in the things of this world.
Reflect on what it would mean to let the bread
of life satisfy all your hunger and thirst.*

_____

_____

_____

_____

_____

_____

_____

_____

_____

_____

_____

_____

_____

_____

_____

∼ ❀ ∽
DAY 16

John 15:1-5, 8-17

"I am the true vine, and my Father is the vineyard keeper. He removes any of my branches that don't produce fruit, and he trims any branch that produces fruit so that it will produce even more fruit. You are already trimmed because of the word I have spoken to you. Remain in me, and I will remain in you. A branch can't produce fruit by itself, but must remain in the vine. Likewise, you can't produce fruit unless you remain in me. I am the vine; you are the branches. If you remain in me and I in you, then you will produce much fruit. Without me, you can't do anything. My Father is glorified when you produce much fruit and in this way prove that you are my disciples.

"As the Father loved me, I too have loved you. Remain in my love. If you keep my commandments, you will remain in my love, just as I kept my Father's commandments and remain in his love. I have said these things to you so that my joy will be in you and your joy will be complete. This is my commandment: love each other just as I have loved you. No one has greater love than to give up one's life for one's friends. You are my friends if you do what I command you. I don't call you servants any longer, because servants don't know what their master is doing. Instead, I call you friends, because everything I heard from my Father I have made known to you. You didn't choose me, but I chose you and appointed you so that you could go and produce fruit and so that your fruit could last. As a result, whatever you ask the Father in my name, he will give you. I give you these commandments so that you can love each other."

Colossians 1:10-14

We're praying this so that you can live lives that are worthy of the Lord and pleasing to him in every way: by producing fruit in every good work and growing in the knowledge of God; by being strengthened through his glorious might so that you endure everything and have patience; and by giving thanks with joy to the Father. He made it so you could take part in the inheritance, in light granted to God's holy people. He rescued us from the control of darkness and transferred us into the kingdom of the Son he loves. He set us free through the Son and forgave our sins.

∽ MEDITATION ∾

God chose us and appointed us to be fruit-bearers. Reflect on the fruit that's coming from your life. Are hope, joy, and love among the fruits you are bearing?

DAY 17

Matthew 11:28-30

"Come to me, all you who are struggling hard and carrying heavy loads, and I will give you rest. Put on my yoke, and learn from me. I'm gentle and humble. And you will find rest for yourselves. My yoke is easy to bear, and my burden is light."

Genesis 2:2-3

On the sixth day God completed all the work that he had done, and on the seventh day God rested from all the work that he had done. God blessed the seventh day and made it holy, because on it God rested from all the work of creation.

Isaiah 40:26-31

Look up at the sky and consider:
 Who created these?
 The one who brings out their attendants one by one,
 summoning each of them by name.

Because of God's great strength
  and mighty power, not one is missing.
Why do you say, Jacob, and declare, Israel,
  "My way is hidden from the LORD,
  my God ignores my predicament"?
Don't you know? Haven't you heard?
  The LORD is the everlasting God,
  the creator of the ends of the earth.
  He doesn't grow tired or weary.
His understanding is beyond human reach,
  giving power to the tired
  and reviving the exhausted.
Youths will become tired and weary,
  young men will certainly stumble;
  but those who hope in the LORD
    will renew their strength;
  they will fly up on wings like eagles;
  they will run and not be tired;
  they will walk and not be weary.

Psalm 37:3-7

Trust the LORD and do good;
  live in the land, and farm faithfulness.
Enjoy the LORD,
  and he will give what your heart asks.
Commit your way to the LORD!
  Trust him! He will act
  and will make your righteousness shine
    like the dawn,
  your justice like high noon.

Be still before the LORD,
and wait for him.
Don't get upset when someone gets ahead—
someone who invents evil schemes.

MEDITATION

*We know that our God gives power to the tired
and revives the exhausted. How can you find
rest and let the Lord restore your strength?*

_____

_____

_____

_____

_____

_____

_____

_____

_____

_____

DAY 18

Romans 8:15-18

You didn't receive a spirit of slavery to lead you back again into fear, but you received a Spirit that shows you are adopted as his children. With this Spirit, we cry, "Abba, Father." The same Spirit agrees with our spirit, that we are God's children. But if we are children, we are also heirs. We are God's heirs and fellow heirs with Christ, if we really suffer with him so that we can also be glorified with him.

I believe that the present suffering is nothing compared to the coming glory that is going to be revealed to us.

Matthew 6:25-34

"Therefore, I say to you, don't worry about your life, what you'll eat or what you'll drink, or about your body, what you'll wear. Isn't life more than food and the body more than clothes? Look at the birds in the sky. They don't sow seed or harvest grain or gather crops into barns. Yet your heavenly Father feeds them. Aren't you worth much more than they are? Who among you by worrying can add a single moment to your life? And why do you worry about clothes? Notice how the lilies in the field grow. They don't wear themselves out with work, and they don't spin cloth. But I say to you that even Solomon in all of his splendor wasn't dressed like one of these. If God dresses grass in the field so beautifully, even though it's alive today and tomorrow it's thrown into the furnace, won't God do much more for you, you people of weak faith? Therefore, don't worry and say, 'What are we going to eat?' or 'What are we going to drink?' or 'What are we going to wear?' Gentiles long for all these things. Your heavenly Father knows that you need them. Instead, desire first and foremost God's kingdom and God's righteousness, and all these things will be given to you as well. Therefore, stop worrying about tomorrow, because tomorrow will worry about itself. Each day has enough trouble of its own."

1 John 4:9-10

This is how the love of God is revealed to us: God has sent his only Son into the world so that we can live through him. This is love: it is not that we loved God but that he loved us and sent his Son as the sacrifice that deals with our sins.

MEDITATION

What joy we have in being the children of God.
Spend time meditating on God's heart,
and write down some of the promises
we have as God's children.

Day 19

John 16:5-11

"But now I go away to the one who sent me. None of you ask me, 'Where are you going?' Yet because I have said these things to you, you are filled with sorrow. I assure you that it is better for you that I go away. If I don't go away, the Companion won't come to you. But if I go, I will send him to you. When he comes, he will show the world it was wrong about sin, righteousness, and judgment. He will show the world it was wrong about sin because they don't believe in me. He will show the world it was wrong about righteousness because I'm going to the Father and you won't see me anymore. He will show the world it was wrong about judgment because this world's ruler stands condemned."

Romans 8:11

If the Spirit of the one who raised Jesus from the dead lives in you, the one who raised Christ from the dead will give life to your human bodies also, through his Spirit that lives in you.

Ephesians 1:7-14

We have been ransomed through his Son's blood, and we have forgiveness for our failures based on his overflowing grace, which he poured over us with wisdom and understanding. God revealed his hidden design to us, which is according to his goodwill and the plan that he intended to accomplish through his Son. This is what God planned for the climax of all times: to bring all things together in Christ, the things in heaven along with the things on earth. We have also received an inheritance in Christ. We were destined by the plan of God, who accomplishes everything according to his design. We are called to be an honor to God's glory because we were the first to hope in Christ. You too heard the word of truth in Christ, which is the good news of your salvation. You were sealed with the promised Holy Spirit because you believed in Christ. The Holy Spirit is the down payment on our inheritance, which is applied toward our redemption as God's own people, resulting in the honor of God's glory.

MEDITATION

God has sent us the Holy Spirit. Where do you see the Spirit at work in your life? How can we let the Spirit be the source of our hope?

DAY 20

Matthew 16:13-20

Now when Jesus came to the area of Caesarea Philippi, he asked his disciples, "Who do people say the Human One is?"

They replied, "Some say John the Baptist, others Elijah, and still others Jeremiah or one of the other prophets."

He said, "And what about you? Who do you say that I am?"

Simon Peter said, "You are the Christ, the Son of the living God."

Then Jesus replied, "Happy are you, Simon son of Jonah, because no human has shown this to you. Rather my Father who is in heaven has shown you. I tell you that you are Peter. And I'll build my church on this rock. The gates of the underworld won't be able to stand against it. I'll give you the keys of the kingdom of heaven. Anything you fasten on earth will be fastened in heaven. Anything you loosen on earth will be loosened in heaven." Then he ordered the disciples not to tell anybody that he was the Christ.

Colossians 3:12-17

Therefore, as God's choice, holy and loved, put on compassion, kindness, humility, gentleness, and patience. Be tolerant with each other and, if someone has a complaint against anyone, forgive each other. As the Lord forgave you, so also forgive each other. And over all these things put on love, which is the perfect bond of unity. The peace of Christ must control your hearts—a peace into which you were called in one body. And be thankful people. The word of Christ must live in you richly. Teach and warn each other with all wisdom by singing psalms, hymns, and spiritual songs. Sing to God with gratitude in your hearts. Whatever you do, whether in speech or action, do it all in the name of the Lord Jesus and give thanks to God the Father through him.

MEDITATION

We have clear instructions about how to be in unity with each other and how to be the church, but we don't always follow them so well. Write a list of ways that being a part of the body of Christ strengthens your hope.

_____

_____

_____

_____

DAY 21

Luke 19:29-38

As Jesus came to Bethphage and Bethany on the Mount of Olives, he gave two disciples a task. He said, "Go into the village over there. When you enter it, you will find tied up there a colt that no one has ever ridden. Untie it and bring it here. If someone asks, 'Why are you untying it?' just say, 'Its master needs it.'" Those who had been sent found it exactly as he had said.

As they were untying the colt, its owners said to them, "Why are you untying the colt?"

They replied, "Its master needs it." They brought it to Jesus, threw their clothes on the colt, and lifted Jesus onto it. As Jesus rode along, they spread their clothes on the road.

As Jesus approached the road leading down from the Mount of Olives, the whole throng of his disciples began rejoicing. They praised God with a loud voice because of all the mighty things they had seen. They said,

"Blessings on the king who comes in the name
of the Lord.
Peace in heaven and glory in the highest heavens."

John 4:19-24

The woman said, "Sir, I see that you are a prophet. Our ancestors worshipped on this mountain, but you and your people say that it is necessary to worship in Jerusalem."

Jesus said to her, "Believe me, woman, the time is coming when you and your people will worship the Father neither on this mountain nor in Jerusalem. You and your people worship what you don't know; we worship what we know because salvation is from the Jews. But the time is coming—and is here!—when true worshippers will worship in spirit and truth. The Father looks for those who worship him this way. God is spirit, and it is necessary to worship God in spirit and truth."

Psalm 95:1-5

Come, let's sing out loud to the LORD!
  Let's raise a joyful shout to the rock of our salvation!
Let's come before him with thanks!
  Let's shout songs of joy to him!
The LORD is a great God,
  the great king over all other gods.
The earth's depths are in his hands;
  the mountain heights belong to him;
  the sea, which he made, is his
    along with the dry ground,
    which his own hands formed.

MEDITATION

In your own life, how are you worshipping God in spirit and in truth? How can you joyfully worship God in spirit and truth?

_____

_____

_____

_____

_____

_____

_____

_____

_____

_____

_____

_____

_____

_____

_____

Day 22

Psalm 74:16-17

The day belongs to you! The night too!
You established both the moon and the sun.
You set all the boundaries of the earth in place.
Summer and winter? You made them!

Ecclesiastes 3:1-8

There's a season for everything
    and a time for every matter under the heavens:
    a time for giving birth and a time for dying,
    a time for planting and a time for uprooting
        what was planted,
    a time for killing and a time for healing,
    a time for tearing down and a time for building up,
    a time for crying and a time for laughing,
    a time for mourning and a time for dancing,
    a time for throwing stones
        and a time for gathering stones,
    a time for embracing
        and a time for avoiding embraces,
    a time for searching and a time for losing,

a time for keeping and a time for throwing away,
a time for tearing and a time for repairing,
a time for keeping silent and a time for speaking,
a time for loving and a time for hating,
a time for war and a time for peace.

Psalm 1:1-3

The truly happy person
  doesn't follow wicked advice,
  doesn't stand on the road of sinners,
  and doesn't sit with the disrespectful.
Instead of doing those things,
  these persons love the LORD's Instruction,
  and they recite God's Instruction day and night!
They are like a tree replanted by streams of water,
  which bears fruit at just the right time
  and whose leaves don't fade.
    Whatever they do succeeds.

Song of Songs 2:12-13

Blossoms have appeared in the land;
  the season of singing has arrived,
  and the sound of the turtledove is heard in our land.
The green fruit is on the fig tree,
  and the grapevines in bloom are fragrant.
Rise up, my dearest,
  my fairest, and go.

MEDITATION

There is a season for everything. Reflect on what season of life you are in now. How can you find hope in this season and in all seasons?

_____

_____

_____

_____

_____

_____

_____

_____

_____

_____

_____

_____

_____

_____

_____

_____

_____

Day 23

John 11:17-27

When Jesus arrived, he found that Lazarus had already been in the tomb for four days. Bethany was a little less than two miles from Jerusalem. Many Jews had come to comfort Martha and Mary after their brother's death. When Martha heard that Jesus was coming, she went to meet him, while Mary remained in the house. Martha said to Jesus, "Lord, if you had been here, my brother wouldn't have died. Even now I know that whatever you ask God, God will give you."

Jesus told her, "Your brother will rise again."

Martha replied, "I know that he will rise in the resurrection on the last day."

Jesus said to her, "I am the resurrection and the life. Whoever believes in me will live, even though they die. Everyone who lives and believes in me will never die. Do you believe this?"

She replied, "Yes, Lord, I believe that you are the Christ, God's Son, the one who is coming into the world."

Romans 8:28-30

We know that God works all things together for good for the ones who love God, for those who are called according to his purpose. We know this because God knew them in advance, and he decided in advance that they would be conformed to the image of his Son. That way his Son would be the first of many brothers and sisters. Those who God decided in advance would be conformed to his Son, he also called. Those whom he called, he also made righteous. Those whom he made righteous, he also glorified.

Hebrews 10:19-23

Brothers and sisters, we have confidence that we can enter the holy of holies by means of Jesus' blood, through a new and living way that he opened up for us through the curtain, which is his body, and we have a great high priest over God's house.

Therefore, let's draw near with a genuine heart with the certainty that our faith gives us, since our hearts are sprinkled clean from an evil conscience and our bodies are washed with pure water.

Let's hold on to the confession of our hope without wavering, because the one who made the promises is reliable.

Romans 4:20-21

He didn't hesitate with a lack of faith in God's promise, but he grew strong in faith and gave glory to God. He was fully convinced that God was able to do what he promised.

MEDITATION

Are you fully convinced that God is able to do what has been promised? Spend time reading some promises that God has made in scripture. How do they make you feel? Hopeful? Joyful? Expectant?

_____

_____

_____

_____

_____

_____

_____

_____

_____

DAY 24

John 13:1-12

Before the Festival of Passover, Jesus knew that his time had come to leave this world and go to the Father. Having loved his own who were in the world, he loved them fully.

Jesus and his disciples were sharing the evening meal. The devil had already provoked Judas, Simon Iscariot's son, to betray Jesus. Jesus knew the Father had given everything into his hands and that he had come from God and was returning to God. So he got up from the table and took off his robes. Picking up a linen towel, he tied it around his waist. Then he poured water into a washbasin and began to wash the disciples' feet, drying them with the towel he was wearing. When Jesus came to Simon Peter, Peter said to him, "Lord, are you going to wash my feet?"

Jesus replied, "You don't understand what I'm doing now, but you will understand later."

"No!" Peter said. "You will never wash my feet!"

Jesus replied, "Unless I wash you, you won't have a place with me."

Simon Peter said, "Lord, not only my feet but also my hands and my head!"

Jesus responded, "Those who have bathed need only to have their feet washed, because they are completely clean. You disciples are clean, but not every one of you." He knew who would betray him. That's why he said, "Not every one of you is clean."

After he washed the disciples' feet, he put on his robes and returned to his place at the table. He said to them, "Do you know what I've done for you?"

Philippians 2:1-3

Therefore, if there is any encouragement in Christ, any comfort in love, any sharing in the Spirit, any sympathy, complete my joy by thinking the same way, having the same love, being united, and agreeing with each other. Don't do anything for selfish purposes, but with humility think of others as better than yourselves.

MEDITATION

We can complete the joy of Jesus
by being humble. Reflect on how you
can wash somebody else's feet today,
just as Jesus humbled himself
and washed the feet of the disciples.

John 19:17-30

Carrying his cross by himself, he went out to a place called Skull Place (in Aramaic, *Golgotha*). That's where they crucified him—and two others with him, one on each side and Jesus in the middle. Pilate had a public notice written and posted on the cross. It read "Jesus the Nazarene, the king of the Jews." Many of the Jews read this sign, for the place where Jesus was crucified was near the city and it was written in Aramaic, Latin, and Greek. Therefore, the Jewish chief priests complained to Pilate, "Don't write, 'The king of the Jews' but 'This man said, "I am the king of the Jews."'"

Pilate answered, "What I've written, I've written."

When the soldiers crucified Jesus, they took his clothes and his sandals, and divided them into four shares, one for each soldier. His shirt was seamless, woven as one piece from the top to the bottom. They said to each other, "Let's not tear it. Let's cast lots to see who will get it." This was to fulfill the scripture,

They divided my clothes among themselves,
and they cast lots for my clothing.

That's what the soldiers did.

Jesus' mother and his mother's sister, Mary the wife of Clopas, and Mary Magdalene stood near the cross. When Jesus saw his mother and the disciple whom he loved standing nearby, he said to his mother, "Woman, here is your son." Then he said to the disciple, "Here is your mother." And from that time on, this disciple took her into his home.

After this, knowing that everything was already completed, in order to fulfill the scripture, Jesus said, "I am thirsty." A jar full of sour wine was nearby, so the soldiers soaked a sponge in it, placed it on a hyssop branch, and held it up to his lips. When he had received the sour wine, Jesus said, "It is completed." Bowing his head, he gave up his life.

1 Corinthians 1:18

The message of the cross is foolishness to those who are being destroyed. But it is the power of God for those of us who are being saved.

Hebrews 12:1-2

So then let's also run the race that is laid out in front of us, since we have such a great cloud of witnesses surrounding us. Let's throw off any extra baggage, get rid of the sin that trips us up, and fix our eyes on Jesus, faith's pioneer and perfecter. He endured the cross, ignoring the shame, for the sake of the joy that was laid out in front of him, and sat down at the right side of God's throne.

MEDITATION

What meaning do you take from the passage in Hebrews that says, "He endured the cross, ignoring the shame, for the sake of the joy that was laid out in front of him"? What does this teach us about hope?

_____

_____

_____

_____

_____

_____

_____

_____

_____

_____

_____

_____

_____

DAY 26

2 Samuel 22:1-7

David spoke the words of this song to the LORD after the LORD delivered him from the power of all his enemies and from Saul.

He said:

The LORD is my solid rock, my fortress, my rescuer.
My God is my rock—I take refuge in him!—
he's my shield and my salvation's strength,
my place of safety and my shelter.
My savior! Save me from violence!
Because he is praiseworthy,
I cried out to the LORD,
and I was saved from my enemies.
Death's waves were all around me;
rivers of wickedness terrified me.
The cords of the grave surrounded me;
death's traps held me tight.
In my distress I cried out to the LORD;
I cried out to my God.
God heard my voice from his temple;
my cry for help reached his ears.

2 Chronicles 5:12-14

All the levitical musicians—Asaph, Heman, Jeduthun, and their families and relatives—were dressed in fine linen and stood east of the altar with cymbals, harps, and zithers, along with one hundred twenty priests blowing trumpets. The trumpeters and singers joined together to praise and thank the LORD as one. Accompanied by trumpets, cymbals, and other musical instruments, they began to sing, praising the LORD:

Yes, God is good!
Yes, God's faithful love lasts forever!

Then a cloud filled the LORD's temple. The priests were unable to carry out their duties on account of the cloud because the LORD's glory filled God's temple.

Psalm 98:1-6

Sing to the LORD a new song
because he has done wonderful things!
His own strong hand and his own holy arm
have won the victory!
The LORD has made his salvation widely known;
he has revealed his righteousness
in the eyes of all the nations.
God has remembered his loyal love
and faithfulness to the house of Israel;
every corner of the earth has seen
our God's salvation.
Shout triumphantly to the LORD, all the earth!

Be happy!
Rejoice out loud!
Sing your praises!
Sing your praises to the LORD with the lyre—
with the lyre and the sound of music.
With trumpets and a horn blast,
shout triumphantly before the LORD, the king!

MEDITATION

*All throughout the Bible we see people
expressing joy, thanksgiving, and hope for the
Lord in song. How do you express your hope,
thanksgiving, and joy for God?*

_____

_____

_____

_____

_____

_____

_____

_____

DAY 27

Luke 15:8-10

"Or what woman, if she owns ten silver coins and loses one of them, won't light a lamp and sweep the house, searching her home carefully until she finds it? When she finds it, she calls together her friends and neighbors, saying, 'Celebrate with me because I've found my lost coin.' In the same way, I tell you, joy breaks out in the presence of God's angels over one sinner who changes both heart and life."

Nehemiah 8:8-12

They read aloud from the scroll, the Instruction from God, explaining and interpreting it so the people could understand what they heard.

Then Nehemiah the governor, Ezra the priest and scribe, and the Levites who taught the people said to all of the people, "This day is holy to the LORD your God. Don't mourn or weep." They said this because all the people wept when they heard the words of the Instruction.

"Go, eat rich food, and drink something sweet," he said to them, "and send portions of this to any who have nothing ready! This day is holy to our LORD. Don't be sad, because the joy from the LORD is your strength!"

The Levites also calmed all of the people, saying, "Be quiet, for this day is holy. Don't be sad!" Then all of the people went to eat and to drink, to send portions, and to have a great celebration, because they understood what had been said to them.

Psalm 149:4

Because the LORD is pleased with his people,
God will beautify the poor with saving help.

∽ MEDITATION ∼

Do the things that God delights in bring you hope? Reflect on what it truly means for the joy of the Lord to be your strength.

_____

_____

_____

_____

_____

DAY 28

1 Thessalonians 5:16-18

Rejoice always. Pray continually. Give thanks in every situation because this is God's will for you in Christ Jesus.

Psalm 118:1-4

Give thanks to the LORD because he is good,
　because his faithful love lasts forever.
Let Israel say it:
　"God's faithful love lasts forever!"
Let the house of Aaron say it:
　"God's faithful love lasts forever!"
Let those who honor the LORD say it:
　"God's faithful love lasts forever!"

Romans 1:20-21

Ever since the creation of the world, God's invisible qualities—God's eternal power and divine nature—have been clearly seen, because they are understood through the things God has made. So humans are without excuse. Although they knew God, they didn't honor God as God or thank him. Instead, their reasoning became pointless, and their foolish hearts were darkened.

Psalm 100:1-5

Shout triumphantly to the LORD, all the earth!
  Serve the LORD with celebration!
  Come before him with shouts of joy!
Know that the LORD is God—
  he made us; we belong to him.
  We are his people,
  the sheep of his own pasture.
Enter his gates with thanks;
  enter his courtyards with praise!
  Thank him! Bless his name!
Because the LORD is good,
  his loyal love lasts forever;
  his faithfulness lasts generation after generation.

MEDITATION

Practicing a thankful heart yields a hopeful heart. What are you thankful for today? How does this give you hope?

Day 28

DAY 29

Luke 16:10-15

"Whoever is faithful with little is also faithful with much, and the one who is dishonest with little is also dishonest with much. If you haven't been faithful with worldly wealth, who will trust you with true riches? If you haven't been faithful with someone else's property, who will give you your own? No household servant can serve two masters. Either you will hate the one and love the other, or you will be loyal to the one and have contempt for the other. You cannot serve God and wealth."

The Pharisees, who were money-lovers, heard all this and sneered at Jesus. He said to them, "You are the ones who justify yourselves before other people, but God knows your hearts. What is highly valued by people is deeply offensive to God."

Matthew 6:19-21

"Stop collecting treasures for your own benefit on earth, where moth and rust eat them and where thieves break in and steal them. Instead, collect treasures for yourselves in heaven, where moth and rust don't eat them and where thieves don't break in and steal them. Where your treasure is, there your heart will be also."

2 Corinthians 1:12

We have conducted ourselves with godly sincerity and pure motives in the world, and especially toward you. This is why we are confident, and our conscience confirms this. We didn't act with human wisdom but we relied on the grace of God.

Matthew 18:1-5

At that time the disciples came to Jesus and asked, "Who is the greatest in the kingdom of heaven?"

Then he called a little child over to sit among the disciples, and said, "I assure you that if you don't turn your lives around and become like this little child, you will definitely not enter the kingdom of heaven. Those who humble themselves like this little child will be the greatest in the kingdom of heaven. Whoever welcomes one such child in my name welcomes me."

MEDITATION

Where might God be calling you to simplify?
How can we embrace simplicity rather
than abundance or complexity?

_____

_____

_____

_____

_____

_____

_____

_____

_____

_____

_____

_____

_____

_____

_____

_____

_____

DAY 30

Jeremiah 29:10-14

The LORD proclaims: When Babylon's seventy years are up, I will come and fulfill my gracious promise to bring you back to this place. I know the plans I have in mind for you, declares the LORD; they are plans for peace, not disaster, to give you a future filled with hope. When you call me and come and pray to me, I will listen to you. When you search for me, yes, search for me with all your heart, you will find me. I will be present for you, declares the LORD, and I will end your captivity. I will gather you from all the nations and places where I have scattered you, and I will bring you home after your long exile declares the LORD.

John 4:4-14

Jesus had to go through Samaria. He came to a Samaritan city called Sychar, which was near the land Jacob had given to his son Joseph. Jacob's well was there. Jesus was tired from his journey, so he sat down at the well. It was about noon.

A Samaritan woman came to the well to draw water. Jesus said to her, "Give me some water to drink." His disciples had gone into the city to buy him some food.

The Samaritan woman asked, "Why do you, a Jewish man, ask for something to drink from me, a Samaritan woman?" (Jews and Samaritans didn't associate with each other.)

Jesus responded, "If you recognized God's gift and who is saying to you, 'Give me some water to drink,' you would be asking him and he would give you living water."

The woman said to him, "Sir, you don't have a bucket and the well is deep. Where would you get this living water? You aren't greater than our father Jacob, are you? He gave this well to us, and he drank from it himself, as did his sons and his livestock."

Jesus answered, "Everyone who drinks this water will be thirsty again, but whoever drinks from the water that I will give will never be thirsty again. The water that I give will become in those who drink it a spring of water that bubbles up into eternal life."

MEDITATION

There is great hope in the journey.
What can we take away from the story
of Jesus' journey through Samaria?

_____

_____

_____

_____

DAY 31

Proverbs 21:15

Acting justly is a joy to the righteous,
but dreaded by those who do evil.

Isaiah 61:8-9

I, the LORD, love justice;
I hate robbery and dishonesty.
I will faithfully give them their wage,
and make with them an enduring covenant.
Their offspring will be known among the nations,
and their descendants among the peoples.
All who see them will recognize
that they are a people blessed by the LORD.

Psalm 37:3-8

Trust the LORD and do good;
live in the land, and farm faithfulness.

Enjoy the LORD,
  and he will give what your heart asks.
Commit your way to the LORD!
    Trust him! He will act
    and will make your righteousness shine like the dawn,
    your justice like high noon.
Be still before the LORD,
  and wait for him.
Don't get upset when someone gets ahead—
    someone who invents evil schemes.
Let go of anger and leave rage behind!
    Don't get upset—it will only lead to evil.

Isaiah 51:4-5

Pay attention to me, my people;
  listen to me, my nation,
    for teaching will go out from me,
    my justice, as a light to the nations.
  I will quickly bring my victory.
My salvation is on its way,
  and my arm will judge the peoples.
  The coastlands hope for me;
  they wait for my judgment.

Isaiah 1:17

Learn to do good.
Seek justice:
  help the oppressed;
  defend the orphan;
  plead for the widow.

MEDITATION

*God loves justice. How might God be
calling you to work for justice?*

_____

_____

_____

_____

_____

_____

_____

_____

_____

_____

_____

Day 32

Genesis 1:1-9

When God began to create the heavens and the earth—the earth was without shape or form, it was dark over the deep sea, and God's wind swept over the waters—God said, "Let there be light." And so light appeared. God saw how good the light was. God separated the light from the darkness. God named the light Day and the darkness Night.

There was evening and there was morning: the first day.

God said, "Let there be a dome in the middle of the waters to separate the waters from each other." God made the dome and separated the waters under the dome from the waters above the dome. And it happened in that way. God named the dome Sky.

There was evening and there was morning: the second day.

God said, "Let the waters under the sky come together into one place so that the dry land can appear." And that's what happened.

Psalm 95:3-5

The LORD is a great God,
  the great king over all other gods.

The earth's depths are in his hands;
  the mountain heights belong to him;
  the sea, which he made, is his
    along with the dry ground,
    which his own hands formed.

Job 12:7-10

But ask Behemoth, and he will teach you,
  the birds in the sky, and they will tell you;
  or talk to earth, and it will teach you;
  the fish of the sea will recount it for you.
Among all these, who hasn't known
  that the LORD's hand did this?
In whose grasp is the life of every thing,
  the breath of every person?

MEDITATION

Take a look around you at the beauty of God's handiwork. What do you experience when you sit and soak in the majesty of God's creation?

_____

_____

DAY 33

Psalm 139:13-18

You are the one who created my innermost parts;
  you knit me together while I was still
    in my mother's womb.
I give thanks to you that I was marvelously set apart.
  Your works are wonderful—I know that very well.
My bones weren't hidden from you
  when I was being put together in a secret place,
  when I was being woven together
    in the deep parts of the earth.
Your eyes saw my embryo,
  and on your scroll every day was written
    that was being formed for me,
  before any one of them had yet happened.
God, your plans are incomprehensible to me!
  Their total number is countless!
If I tried to count them—
  they outnumber grains of sand!
  If I came to the very end—I'd still be with you.

Genesis 1:26-27

Then God said, "Let us make humanity in our image to resemble us so that they may take charge of the fish of the sea, the birds in the sky, the livestock, all the earth, and all the crawling things on earth."

God created humanity in God's own image,
in the divine image God created them,
male and female God created them.

Romans 5:6-11

While we were still weak, at the right moment, Christ died for ungodly people. It isn't often that someone will die for a righteous person, though maybe someone might dare to die for a good person. But God shows his love for us, because while we were still sinners Christ died for us. So, now that we have been made righteous by his blood, we can be even more certain that we will be saved from God's wrath through him. If we were reconciled to God through the death of his Son while we were still enemies, now that we have been reconciled, how much more certain is it that we will be saved by his life? And not only that: we even take pride in God through our Lord Jesus Christ, the one through whom we now have a restored relationship with God.

MEDITATION

*In our humanity we are weak and imperfect
beings. Even still, how does knowing
we were made in the divine image
of God bring us hope and joy?*

_____

_____

_____

_____

_____

_____

_____

_____

_____

_____

_____

_____

_____

Day 34

Proverbs 12:15

Fools see their own way as right,
but the wise listen to advice.

Proverbs 3:13-20

Happy are those who find wisdom
and those who gain understanding.
Her profit is better than silver,
and her gain better than gold.
Her value exceeds pearls;
all you desire can't compare with her.
In her right hand is a long life;
in her left are wealth and honor.
Her ways are pleasant;
all her paths are peaceful.
She is a tree of life to those who embrace her;
those who hold her tight are happy.
The LORD laid the foundations of the earth with wisdom,
establishing the heavens with understanding.
With his knowledge, the watery depths burst open,
and the skies drop dew.

Proverbs 19:20-21

Listen to advice and accept instruction,
    so you might grow wise in the future.
Many plans are in a person's mind,
    but the LORD's purpose will succeed.

Hebrews 4:11-16

Therefore, let's make every effort to enter that rest so that no one will fall by following the same example of disobedience, because God's word is living, active, and sharper than any two-edged sword. It penetrates to the point that it separates the soul from the spirit and the joints from the marrow. It's able to judge the heart's thoughts and intentions. No creature is hidden from it, but rather everything is naked and exposed to the eyes of the one to whom we have to give an answer.

Also, let's hold on to the confession since we have a great high priest who passed through the heavens, who is Jesus, God's Son; because we don't have a high priest who can't sympathize with our weaknesses but instead one who was tempted in every way that we are, except without sin.

Finally, let's draw near to the throne of favor with confidence so that we can receive mercy and find grace when we need help.

MEDITATION

Proverbs tells us, "Happy are those who find wisdom." Where in your life are you seeking wisdom? How are you responding to this wisdom?

_____

_____

_____

_____

_____

_____

_____

_____

_____

_____

_____

_____

_____

_____

DAY 35

1 John 4:7-19

Dear friends, let's love each other, because love is from God, and everyone who loves is born from God and knows God. The person who doesn't love does not know God, because God is love. This is how the love of God is revealed to us: God has sent his only Son into the world so that we can live through him. This is love: it is not that we loved God but that he loved us and sent his Son as the sacrifice that deals with our sins.

Dear friends, if God loved us this way, we also ought to love each other. No one has ever seen God. If we love each other, God remains in us and his love is made perfect in us. This is how we know we remain in him and he remains in us, because he has given us a measure of his Spirit. We have seen and testify that the Father has sent the Son to be the savior of the world. If any of us confess that Jesus is God's Son, God remains in us and we remain in God. We have known and have believed the love that God has for us.

God is love, and those who remain in love remain in God and God remains in them. This is how love has been perfected in us, so that we can have confidence on the Judgment Day, because we are exactly the same as God is in this world. There is no fear in love, but perfect love drives out fear, because fear expects punishment. The person who is afraid has not been made perfect in love. We love because God first loved us.

1 Corinthians 13:3-7

If I give away everything that I have and hand over my own body to feel good about what I've done but I don't have love, I receive no benefit whatsoever.

Love is patient, love is kind, it isn't jealous, it doesn't brag, it isn't arrogant, it isn't rude, it doesn't seek its own advantage, it isn't irritable, it doesn't keep a record of complaints, it isn't happy with injustice, but it is happy with the truth. Love puts up with all things, trusts in all things, hopes for all things, endures all things.

MEDITATION

The Bible gives a beautiful depiction of love:
perfect love drives out fear. Are you
joyfully and fearlessly loving God?
Are you joyfully and fearlessly loving people?
How can you grow in your love?

DAY 36

Titus 3:4-8

But "when God our savior's kindness and love appeared, he saved us because of his mercy, not because of righteous things we had done. He did it through the washing of new birth and the renewing by the Holy Spirit, which God poured out upon us generously through Jesus Christ our savior. So, since we have been made righteous by his grace, we can inherit the hope for eternal life." This saying is reliable. And I want you to insist on these things, so that those who have come to believe in God might give careful attention to doing good. These things are good and useful for everyone.

Ephesians 2:1-7

At one time you were like a dead person because of the things you did wrong and your offenses against God. You used to live like people of this world. You followed the rule of a destructive spiritual power. This is the spirit of disobedience to God's will that is now at work in persons whose lives are characterized by disobedience. At one time you were like those persons. All of you used to do whatever felt good and whatever you thought you wanted so that you were children headed for punishment just like everyone else.

However, God is rich in mercy. He brought us to life with Christ while we were dead as a result of those things that we did wrong. He did this because of the great love that he has for us. You are saved by God's grace! And God raised us up and seated us in the heavens with Christ Jesus. God did this to show future generations the greatness of his grace by the goodness that God has shown us in Christ Jesus.

Psalm 145:7-9

They will rave in celebration of your abundant goodness;
　　they will shout joyfully about your righteousness:
"The LORD is merciful and compassionate,
　　very patient, and full of faithful love.
The LORD is good to everyone and everything;
　　God's compassion extends to all his handiwork!"

MEDITATION

The Lord is rich in mercy. God saved us
because of mercy. Is your life joyfully
shouting about God's mercy and goodness?
Reflect on how you see God's mercy
in your life and around you.

DAY 37

Exodus 34:29-35

Moses came down from Mount Sinai. As he came down from the mountain with the two covenant tablets in his hand, Moses didn't realize that the skin of his face shone brightly because he had been talking with God. When Aaron and all the Israelites saw the skin of Moses' face shining brightly, they were afraid to come near him. But Moses called them closer. So Aaron and all the leaders of the community came back to him, and Moses spoke with them. After that, all the Israelites came near as well, and Moses commanded them everything that the LORD had spoken with him on Mount Sinai. When Moses finished speaking with them, he put a veil over his face. Whenever Moses went into the LORD's presence to speak with him, Moses would take the veil off until he came out again. When Moses came out and told the Israelites what he had been commanded, the Israelites would see that the skin of Moses' face was shining brightly. So Moses would put the veil on his face again until the next time he went in to speak with the LORD.

2 Corinthians 3:12-18

So, since we have such a hope, we act with great confidence. We aren't like Moses, who used to put a veil over his face so that the Israelites couldn't watch the end of what was fading away. But their minds were closed. Right up to the present day the same veil remains when the old covenant is read. The veil is not removed because it is taken away by Christ. Even today, whenever Moses is read, a veil lies over their hearts. But whenever someone turns back to the Lord, the veil is removed. The Lord is the Spirit, and where the Lord's Spirit is, there is freedom. All of us are looking with unveiled faces at the glory of the Lord as if we were looking in a mirror. We are being transformed into that same image from one degree of glory to the next degree of glory. This comes from the Lord, who is the Spirit.

1 Peter 4:13

Instead, rejoice as you share Christ's suffering. You share his suffering now so that you may also have overwhelming joy when his glory is revealed.

MEDITATION

*Are you reflecting the glory of God like
a mirror and being transformed into God's
glorious likeness? Do others see the glory
of the Lord on your face like the Israelites
saw on the face of Moses? Do you see
God's glory in others?*

_____

_____

_____

_____

_____

_____

_____

_____

_____

_____

_____

_____

DAY 38

Matthew 5:1-11

Now when Jesus saw the crowds, he went up a mountain. He sat down and his disciples came to him. He taught them, saying:
　"Happy are people who are hopeless,
　　because the kingdom of heaven is theirs.
　"Happy are people who grieve,
　　because they will be made glad.
　"Happy are people who are humble,
　　because they will inherit the earth.
　"Happy are people who are hungry and thirsty
　　for righteousness, because they will be fed
　　until they are full.
　"Happy are people who show mercy,
　　because they will receive mercy.
　"Happy are people who have pure hearts,
　　because they will see God.
　"Happy are people who make peace,
　　because they will be called God's children.
　"Happy are people whose lives are harassed because
　　they are righteous, because the kingdom
　　of heaven is theirs.
　"Happy are you when people insult you

and harass you and speak all kinds of bad
and false things about you, all because of me."

Luke 18:22-30

When Jesus heard this, he said, "There's one more thing. Sell everything you own and distribute the money to the poor. Then you will have treasure in heaven. And come, follow me." When he heard these words, the man became sad because he was extremely rich.

When Jesus saw this, he said, "It's very hard for the wealthy to enter God's kingdom! It's easier for a camel to squeeze through the eye of a needle than for a rich person to enter God's kingdom."

Those who heard this said, "Then who can be saved?"

Jesus replied, "What is impossible for humans is possible for God."

Peter said, "Look, we left everything we own and followed you."

Jesus said to them, "I assure you that anyone who has left house, husband, wife, brothers, sisters, parents, or children because of God's kingdom will receive many times more in this age and eternal life in the coming age."

MEDITATION

Where in your life are you facing poverty?
Physically? Emotionally? Relationally?
Spiritually? Reflect on the Beatitudes.
How is God be calling you to find joy
and hope in your poverty?

_____

_____

_____

_____

_____

_____

_____

_____

_____

_____

_____

_____

_____

DAY 39

Galatians 3:26-29

You are all God's children through faith in Christ Jesus. All of you who were baptized into Christ have clothed yourselves with Christ. There is neither Jew nor Greek; there is neither slave nor free; nor is there male and female, for you are all one in Christ Jesus. Now if you belong to Christ, then indeed you are Abraham's descendants, heirs according to the promise.

1 Corinthians 12:12-27

Christ is just like the human body—a body is a unit and has many parts; and all the parts of the body are one body, even though there are many. We were all baptized by one Spirit into one body, whether Jew or Greek, or slave or free, and we all were given one Spirit to drink. Certainly the body isn't one part but many. If the foot says, "I'm not part of the body because I'm not a hand," does that mean it's not part of the body? If the ear says, "I'm not part of the body because I'm not an eye," does that mean it's not part of the body? If the whole body were an eye, what would happen to the hearing? And if the whole body were an ear, what would happen to the sense of smell? But as it is, God has placed each one of the parts in the body just like he wanted. If all were one and the same body part, what would happen to the body? But as it is, there are many parts but one body. So the eye can't say to the hand, "I don't need you," or in turn, the head can't say to the feet, "I don't need you." Instead, the parts of the body that people think are the weakest are the most necessary. The parts of the body that we think are less honorable are the ones we honor the most. The private parts of our body that aren't presentable are the ones that are given the most dignity. The parts of our body that are presentable don't need this. But God has put the body together, giving greater honor to the part with less honor so that there won't be division in the body and so the parts might have mutual concern for each other. If one part suffers, all the parts suffer with it; if one part gets the glory, all the parts celebrate with it. You are the body of Christ and parts of each other.

MEDITATION

God takes great joy in the uniqueness of each one of us. Do you find joy in the diversity of those around you? Is our diversity good and hopeful? How can we see diversity as a gift from God?

DAY 40

Genesis 12:1-7

The LORD said to Abram, "Leave your land, your family, and your father's household for the land that I will show you. I will make of you a great nation and will bless you. I will make your name respected, and you will be a blessing.

I will bless those who bless you,
those who curse you I will curse;
all the families of the earth
will be blessed because of you."

Abram left just as the LORD told him, and Lot went with him. Now Abram was 75 years old when he left Haran. Abram took his wife Sarai, his nephew Lot, all of their possessions, and those who became members of their household in Haran; and they set out for the land of Canaan. When they arrived in Canaan, Abram traveled through the land as far as the sacred place at Shechem, at the oak of Moreh. The Canaanites lived in the land at that time. The LORD appeared to Abram and said, "I give this land to your descendants," so Abram built an altar there to the LORD who appeared to him.

2 Kings 18:5-8

Hezekiah trusted in the LORD, Israel's God. There was no one like him among all of Judah's kings—not before him and not after him. He clung to the LORD and never deviated from him. He kept the commandments that the LORD had commanded Moses. The LORD was with Hezekiah; he succeeded at everything he tried. He rebelled against Assyria's king and wouldn't serve him. He struck down the Philistines as far as Gaza and its territories, from watchtower to fortified city.

Exodus 19:3-6

Moses went up to God. The LORD called to him from the mountain, "This is what you should say to Jacob's household and declare to the Israelites: You saw what I did to the Egyptians, and how I lifted you up on eagles' wings and brought you to me. So now, if you faithfully obey me and stay true to my covenant, you will be my most precious possession out of all the peoples, since the whole earth belongs to me. You will be a kingdom of priests for me and a holy nation. These are the words you should say to the Israelites."

John 15:9-11

"As the Father loved me, I too have loved you. Remain in my love. If you keep my commandments, you will remain in my love, just as I kept my Father's commandments and remain in his love. I have said these things to you so that my joy will be in you and your joy will be complete."

MEDITATION

Jesus tells us he loves us. We are to remain in his love, then his joy will be in us and our joy will be complete. What does it mean for our joy to be complete? How have you sensed the joy of Jesus in you? How does God's love give you hope?
